Dorothy M. Stewart is the author of *The Bluffer's Guide to Publishing* (Ravette) and *It's Hard to Hurry When You're a Snail* (Lion), and compiler and editor of *A Book of Graces* (SPCK), *Women of Prayer* (Lion), *Women of Spirit* (Lion) and *The Westminster Collection of Christian Prayers* (Westminster John Knox Press). She is a lay preacher in the United Reformed Church and lives in Halesworth, Suffolk.

PRAYERS FOR
THE NIGHT

Compiled and edited by
Dorothy M. Stewart

First published in Great Britain in 2011

Society for Promoting Christian Knowledge
36 Causton Street
London SW1P 4ST
www.spckpublishing.co.uk

British Library Cataloguing-in-Publication Data
A catalogue record for this book is available from the British Library

ISBN 978–0–281–06237–9

1 3 5 7 9 10 8 6 4 2

Typeset by Graphicraft Ltd, Hong Kong
Printed in Great Britain by Ashford Colour Press

Produced on paper from sustainable forests

Contents

———•◦•———

Contents

Introduction

I used to boast I could sleep anywhere. From the bumpy ground of a Girl Guide campsite in my early teens to the thin mattress in a Nigerian railwaymen's hostel during my travels in West Africa in my twenties, feather-filled French mattresses in my thirties that threatened to close on the sleeper like a Venus flytrap . . . been there, and slept well. But now, sleep can be a problem. Or rather, getting to sleep.

Some of my friends are also suffering from poor sleep and we discuss the various remedies we've heard of, or tried – lavender spray for the pillows, an oatcake before bed, or milk or chamomile tea. But I still find myself lying awake through those early hours of the night and fretting that soon it will be morning, time to face another day and I won't have had enough sleep.

And I'm realizing how many others are lying awake – from worry, stress or illness, and still more are awake or trying to stay awake as they feed a new baby, watch over a sick child, a dying relative or patient, or doing all the myriad things that are necessary in our world to keep things running smoothly and the rest of us safe.

As I researched and collected the prayers for this book, I became aware that our ancestors had a very different attitude to life and sleep. Their prayers for the night were simple and straightforward. They came to God in the realistic understanding that life is short and uncertain and they might not wake up the next morning, so they needed to ask forgiveness for their sins, protection from illness and danger, and then simply entrust themselves to God's care and love.

We who think ourselves more sophisticated, living in a world where medical science has banished most of the ailments that so easily carried away earlier folk, may smile fondly at these prayers – but I think maybe we have much to learn from this simplicity of understanding.

Clearing our consciences and entrusting ourselves to God may not bring the longed-for sleep, but will calm the heart and soothe the soul. And for those who watch or wait, the knowledge of God's abiding presence through the long hours is a true comfort and strength.

So I offer these prayers in the hope that they will bless you, whether you want to sleep or stay awake.

1

At the end of a busy day

———◦•◦———

1 Blessed art thou, O Lord our God, King of the universe, who givest strength to the weary.
The Hebrew Prayer Book

2 Dear God, here I am before you. I'm tired – so tired. I keep wondering what happened to my boundless enthusiasm for the life you've given me. Where did it go? When did I lose it?

In place of my enthusiasm, I feel dried out. Deadened.

I don't feel like your victorious child, God. Why has this happened to me? How did I let this happen? Why did you let it happen?

I know all the right things to say. I know that my strength lies in you, that without you I can do nothing. And yet, here I am, powerless, worn out, and weak.

Let me feel your strength, O God –

- the power of your Holy Spirit filling my weary body,
- the energy of your love flowing through me,
- the joy of your salvation bubbling up through my heart.

Take my weariness, my fatigue, and my heaviness. Lift them from my spirit. Fill me with joy, enthusiasm, and zest for life and the tasks before me.

Help me to see every new day as a perfect gift from you, to be lived fully and powerfully, secure in the knowledge that you will provide me with the strength I need to do this.

(*Take three deep breaths, imagining that each one is bringing in energy and strength.*)

Thank you, O God, for taking this weariness from me. Thank you for restoring my strength.
Patricia Wilson

3 I am tired, Lord,
   too tired to think,
   too tired to pray,
   too tired to do anything.
   Too tired,
   drained of resources,
   'labouring at the oars against a head wind',
   pressed down by a force as strong as the sea.
   Lord of all power and might,
   'your way was through the sea,
   your path through the great waters',
   calm my soul,
   take control,
   Lord of all power and might.
   Rex Chapman

4 May he, who with a calm mind slept in the stern,
   then got up and commanded the winds and
      the sea,
   grant that, while my limbs rest here, weary with
      heavy work,
   my mind may keep vigil with him.
   Lamb of God, who bore all the sins of the world,
   keep my calm rest safe from the enemy.
   Alcuin, 735–804

5 Never weather-beaten sail more willing bent to shore,
  Never tired pilgrim's limbs affected slumber more,
  Than my wearied spirite now longs to fly out of my
      troubled breast:
  O come quickly, sweetest Lord, and take my soul to rest!
  Thomas Campion, 1567–1620

6 O God, you know how I feel, and you know that to-night
  I am so tired that I can hardly stay awake to pray. But,
  before I go to sleep, I must say thank you for to-day and
  I must ask your forgiveness for everything in it that was not
  right.

  Help me now to fall asleep thinking about you, and to
  waken to-morrow to live for you.

  This I ask for your love's sake. Amen.
  William Barclay, 1907–78

7 O Lord, Jesus Christ, Who art as the Shadow of a Great Rock
  in a weary land, Who beholdest thine weak creatures weary
  of labour, weary of pleasure, weary of hope deferred, weary
  of self; in Thine abundant compassion, and fellow feeling
  with us, and unutterable tenderness, bring us, we pray thee,
  unto Thy rest . . . Amen.
  Christina Rossetti, 1830–94

8 We come before Thee, O Lord, in the end of thy day with
  thanksgiving.

  Our beloved in the far parts of the earth, those who
  are now beginning the labours of the day what time we end
  them, and those with whom the sun now stands at the point
  of noon, bless, help, console, and prosper them.

  Our guard is relieved, the service of the day is over,
  and the hour come to rest. We resign into thy hands our
  sleeping bodies, our cold hearths, and open doors. Give
  us to awake with smiles, give us to labour smiling. As the

3

sun returns in the east, so let our patience be renewed with dawn; as the sun lightens the world, so let our loving-kindness make bright this house of our habitation.
Robert Louis Stevenson, 1850–94

2

At the end of a happy/special day

————✦————

9 Everything is in its rightful place.
   Everyday concerns are bypassed and put in perspective.
   How light and warm and balanced today has felt.
   Love is restored.
   Thank you.
   Janet Gleadall

10 It's been a lovely day.
      First, breakfast in the garden, bathed in sunshine and
   birdsong and the heavy scent of old-fashioned roses (my
   neighbour's, not mine!).
      Then music which lifted my spirits, followed by meeting
   up with friends – mine and yours – for an afternoon of
   sharing, studying, thinking, talking, praying.
      After supper, back into the garden for an hour's transplant-
   ing, weeding, watering.
      And now, just time to sit quietly in the cool of the late
   evening before bed.
      The sky is drifting into palest grey with chiffon strands
   of sunset pink clouds.
      Blackbird still sings, sweet and clear on the still evening
   air.
      My cat comes out to check on me.
      And I'm at peace and content.
      It's been a lovely day and I know it was Your special gift
   to me,

Your loving blessing –
and I am grateful:
content, and peaceful, and grateful.
Thank You, Lord.
Dorothy M. Stewart

11 Lord, thank you for today and the happiness it has brought
me – not the happiness that wealth or any earthly advance-
ment may bring, but for the simple pleasures that came my
way – the walk through the woods, the warmth of a summer's
day, the light and shadow, the meal with good friends, their
laughter and mine. It has been said, Lord, that happiness
exists only in the past, in remembrance; but today I know
I was happy, and I knew that I loved my life. Thank you
for giving it to me.

This temporal existence will pass, and all my days, happy,
unhappy or a mixture of both, will come to their conclu-
sion; but I know, Lord, that an eternal and unwavering
happiness awaits me – and those I care for – in Your love
and the love of your son Jesus Christ. Amen.
Peter Rowlett

12 Loving God,
our friends have shared our love today
celebrating our wedding,
blessing us with their joy.
Thank you for their love.
So many people have shown their care,
they've worked so quietly on our behalf
to give us this memory.
Thank you for their support.
Their thoughtful presents will help us
build our home together,
a tangible record of this day

and of the special love
with which we are surrounded.
   Thank you for this day.
Rosemary Atkins et al.

13 Thank you, God, for the gift of grandchildren;
   I love them to come and stay.
   And thank you, God, for that blessed peace
   that descends when they've gone away.
   Jean Crowther

14 The house is so quiet now that the children are asleep.
   It has been a great day today,
   and I know that tomorrow is going to be even better.
   Heather Harvey

15 These special dates of special meaning to us
      are ordinary days for others,
   and ordinary days for us
      can be special days for someone else.
   So when we celebrate our anniversaries,
   sometimes others do not know or care.
   It is between us and God.
   The bitter-sweet memories flood in
      and we dare to steep ourselves
      in the sacredness of the day.
   O God,
      thank you for your closeness to us on our special day.
      Thank you that we can celebrate this day of
         remembrance and new beginnings.
      Thank you for those to whom we are linked by love
         for ever and ever.
      Thank you for your love and peace.
   Rosemary Atkins et al.

3

When it's all gone wrong

———•◆•———

16 Be merciful, Lord,
for I am in trouble;
my eyes are sore with crying,
I am exhausted,
I am deep in sorrow,
my life is ebbing away,
my neighbours seem to ignore me,
my friends appear to have forgotten me:
Lord
I trust in you,
I place myself in your care. Amen.
Michael Perry, from Psalm 31

17 Come down, O Christ, and help me!
 Reach Thy hand,
for I am drowning in a stormier sea
than Simon on Thy Lake of Galilee:
the wine of life is spilled upon the sand,
my heart is as some famine-murdered
 land
whence all good things have perished
 utterly,
and well I know my soul in Hell must lie
if I this night before God's throne should
 stand.
Oscar Wilde, 1854–1900

18 Enfold me in Your love,
   I'm so full of hate – give me love.
   I'm so full of anger – give me peace.
   I'm so full of fear – give me trust.
   I cannot go on, Lord. Hold me.
   Anon.

19 I used to feel so sure of you, God, and now I can't find you.
   I can't feel you are there, even when I pray. I don't know
   why it is unless it's because I've let a lot of other things
   crowd my life.
      Please God, let this dark, unhappy time pass. I want to
   find you again – I want to feel you there when I pray. Forgive
   me, and help me to get things straight again.
   Nancy Martin

20 Lord,
   you alone hear my weeping
   and listen to my cry for help:
   don't be angry with me,
   don't punish me.
   I am worn out – have pity on me,
   I am completely exhausted – give me back my strength,
   I am deeply humbled – come and save me.

   Lord, what is the point of it all?
   How long will it be before my prayer is answered?

   Lord, it is in the night that I am so unhappy –
   sometimes my eyes hurt
   and my pillow is wet with tears:
   come to my rescue,
   and drive my enemy away;
   through Jesus my redeemer. Amen.
   Michael Perry, from Psalm 6

21 O God,
    this has been a trying day;
    a day filled with confusion and doubt
    in the midst of love and care.
    There's such a thin line, dear God,
    between being assertive
      and being selfish
    and I've not yet learned to walk that line.
    Help me to keep my balance, God,
    and please pick me up when I fall.
    Jeanne Lischer

22 We cannot see for tears. We cannot even recognize the gentle voice of Jesus: 'Why are you weeping?' Help us in our sorrows to know that he is near, to feel that he cares and even to rejoice in his risen power. In faith may we meet him for he is our Lord, and we love him, Jesus Christ our Saviour. Amen.
    Ian D. Bunting

4

When someone is ill

23 Almighty and everlasting God, the Comfort of the sad, the Strength of sufferers, let the prayers of those that cry out of any tribulation come unto Thee, that all may rejoice to find that Thy mercy is present with them in their afflictions; through Jesus Christ our Lord. Amen.
Gelasian Sacramentary, AD *494*

24 Dear Lord, for all in pain
We pray to Thee;
O come and smite again
Thine enemy.

Give to Thy servants skill
To soothe and bless,
And to the tired and ill
Give quietness.

And, Lord, to those who know
Pain may not cease,
Come near, that even so
They may have peace.
Amy Carmichael, 1867–1951

25 Dear Lord, you know our situation already, but I pray for my (husband/wife/son/daughter, etc.) in hospital at this time, that you will be by his/her side constantly. All that

happens is out of *my* control, but is in *your* control. I pray for the healing of his/her body, and a peace in his/her inner being that you alone can give.

Give wisdom and patience to the doctors and nurses. Restore him/her to health once again I pray. Give me patience as I watch and wait for his/her return home.

In Jesus' Name. Amen.

Beryl White

26 I acknowledge unto thee, O Lord my God and God of my fathers, that both my cure and my death are in thy hands. May it be thy will to send me a perfect healing. Yet if my death be fully determined by thee, I will in love accept it at thy hand . . .

Thou who art the father of the fatherless and judge of the widow, protect my beloved kindred with whose soul my own is knit. Into thy hand I commend my spirit . . . Amen, and Amen!

The Hebrew Prayer Book

27 Lord, the one that I love is sick and in great pain; out of your compassion heal him and take away his pain. It breaks my heart to see him suffer . . . Lord, let him know that you are with him; support and help him that he may come to know you more deeply as a result of his suffering. Lord, be our strength and support in this time of darkness and give us that deep peace which comes from trusting you.

Etta Gullick (adapted)

28 When I lie within my bed,
   sick in heart, and sick in head,
   and with doubts discomforted,
   sweet Spirit comfort me!

When the house doth sigh and weep,
and the world is drawn in sleep,
yet mine eyes the watch do keep;
sweet Spirit comfort me!
Robert Herrick, 1591–1674

5

When you're worried

⸺•⦁•⸺

29 Dear Lord, I'm turning my worries over to you. You're going to be up all night anyway, and I need the sleep! Thank you, Lord. Amen.
Anon.

30 Most loving Lord, give me a childlike love of Thee, which may cast out all fear. Amen.
E. B. Pusey, 1800–82

31 O God, my Father, I worry sometimes at the day's end, when all is quiet:
   I worry about those I love, especially ⸺ and ⸺. Help me to leave them in your love and care, while I do my very best for them. Help me to be sensible about them, and not give way to fussing.
   I worry about my home sometimes, about ⸺ and ⸺. Save me from coveting the things of others, or the advertised good I don't need. Save me from growing casual about the simple joys that once meant much to me.
   I worry about my health sometimes, about ⸺ and ⸺. Enable me to be sensible in the expenditure of my energies. Enable me to take exercise and rest, enough to keep me fresh.
   Bless especially this night all who lack the common decencies of life, all who hunger, all who belong nowhere. Amen.
Rita Snowden, 1907–99

32 O God, our Father, take from our minds this night the worries and anxieties which would keep us from sleeping. Help us to make up our minds bravely to deal with the things which can be dealt with, and not to worry about the things about which we can do nothing.

Take from our hearts this night the feelings which would keep us from resting; take from us all discontent, all envy and jealousy, all vain and useless longings for the things which are not for us.

Take from our bodies the tension which would keep us from relaxing; and help us to lean back in the clasp of the everlasting arms . . .

Hear these our prayers, through Jesus Christ our Lord. Amen.
William Barclay, 1907–78

33 Set free, O Lord, the souls of thy servants from all restlessness and anxiety. Give us that peace and power which flow from thee. Keep us, when in perplexity and distress, that upheld by thy strength and stayed on the rock of thy faithfulness, we may abide in thee, now and for ever.
Francis Paget, 1851–1911

34 This life is so full of worry, Lord. May your peace fill our lives, Heavenly Father, and give us hope for tomorrow. Amen.
Anon.

35 Tonight, as on other nights,
   I'm walking alone
   through the valley of fear.
   O God, I pray
   that You will hear me,
   for you alone know
   what is in my heart.

Lift me out of the valley of despair
and set my soul free.
Northumbria Community

36 You are my Comfort and Duvet.
In the night all my fears surface and my worries loom
    large
as I replay worst case scenarios in my head.
So . . . be with me tonight.
May your presence comfort me,
your love cast out fear
and I cast my worries on to you.

I wrap my duvet tightly around me
to keep me warm, to keep me safe, to keep me snug.
Help me sleep sweetly.
Be my Comfort.
Be my Duvet.
Jonny Baker

6

When you're stressed out and can't switch off

————

37 Lord, I don't know what to say to you tonight. I'm too confused – the prayers I learned off as a child don't mean very much right now. I know you're somewhere in the middle of all this confusion. Please help me to see things more clearly. And be with all those who, like me, don't know what to say to you tonight.
Kairos

38 Lord, the noise of life is oppressing me,
the bother of life obstructing me,
the gossip of life overwhelming.
In the quietness of this evening hour, I ask you to close
    my ears
so I may listen for silence,
close my eyes
so I may see your presence,
close my mouth
so that your words may speak to me clearly.
Calm my body, cleanse my heart,
and rest my soul,
that in waiting on you,
I may rest in you,
peacefully, quietly,
still.
Giles Harcourt

39 O God, help me to-night to relax in body and in mind.

Take from me the tension which makes rest impossible.

Take from me the worries which fill my mind with thoughts which destroy sleep.

Take from me the fears which lurk at the back of my mind, which come to haunt me when work is laid aside, and when there is too much time to think.

Help me to-night really and truly to cast my care upon you, really and truly to feel the everlasting arms underneath and about me.

Help me to sleep to-night, not just the sleep of tiredness, but the sleep of peace; through Jesus Christ my Lord. Amen.
William Barclay, 1907–78

40 O God, you yourself never nod or sleep, but in your wisdom and mercy have given us the gift of sleep. Help me, tonight and every night, to leave my business in your hands, without worry. Let me leave my loved ones and my suffering ones in your safe care. Let me relax and be my real self, taking off my poses with my clothes. Then you can speak to me in the depths of my being and dreams can bring me comfort and wisdom, O Creator of man and Giver of sleep.
George Appleton, 1902–93

41 O Lord, my heart is all a prayer,
But it is silent unto Thee;
I am too tired to look for words,
I rest upon Thy sympathy
To understand when I am dumb,
And well I know Thou hearest me.
Amy Carmichael, 1867–1951

42 This night and every night
seems infinite with questions
and sleep as elusive
as answers.
Pain and longing are always present,
dulled only a little
by the distractions of the day.
I am weary; I am angry.
I am confused.

Circle me, Lord.
Keep despair and disillusion
    without.
Bring a glimmer of hope within.
Circle me, Lord;
keep nightmares without.
Bring moments of rest within.
Circle me, Lord;
keep bitterness without.
Bring a sense
of Your presence within.
Northumbria Community

43 To thee, O God, we turn for peace . . . but grant us too
the blessed assurance that nothing shall deprive us of
that peace, neither ourselves, nor our foolish earthly desires,
nor my wild longings, nor the anxious cravings of my
heart.
Søren Kierkegaard, 1813–55

44 Wearied by the conflict of life, worn by the burden of
the day, we seek Thee as our resting-place. May Thy
eternal calm descend upon our troubled spirits and give
us all Thy peace. Amid the treacherous sands of time

Thou standest still, the Rock of Ages. In life's desert places Thou, O Christ, art a spring whose waters never fail; hear us, we beseech thee, O Lord Christ. Amen.
William Orchard, 1877–1955

7

When you need guidance

45 Be Thou my understanding: thus shall I know that which
it may please Thee that I should know. Nor will I hence-
forth weary myself with seeking: but I will abide in
peace with Thine understanding which shall wholly
occupy my mind. I will not turn my eyes except towards
Love. There will I stay and not move. I see all good to
be in Thee. My spirit can find no place but Thee for its
repose . . . O God! I do not wish to follow Thee for thy
gifts! I want Thyself alone! I want nothing but Thee
alone!
Catherine of Genoa, 1447–1510

46 Christ, I have a new concept of you.
   Suddenly I see you real – not mystical but human – sitting
across from me almost as a doctor would. Instead of a
doctor's face I see yours, the face of the great physician. And
with this comes a marvellous, almost shocking realization:
you can heal me if I will let you.
   I see you too as a wise counsellor. I think of the people
in authority to whom I have turned – a psychologist, a
teacher, a magistrate. Suddenly I am staggered to realize
that you are all of these people in one.
   I don't have to make an appointment, I can turn to
you any time I need. You will listen, you will guide me
about my husband, my children, my job, my very human
concerns.

For you were human too. You are human still. For you live and walk the earth with me and with all these others whom you have made. You understand these awful conflicts.

And so, right now, I lay this latest problem before you. What can I do? You know how desperately I've tried – where have I gone wrong? How can I change this situation?

Even if I cannot hear your counsel, I can feel it. Your strength and your wisdom flow into me. From you, I draw the ability to change what I can, but endure what I must.
Marjorie Holmes

47 Father, you know that I am afraid, and I don't know which way to turn. Please, Lord, come down and comfort me, and help me make the right decisions. Please, Lord, help all those who are going through the same experience as I am. Give them strength through your Holy Spirit. Lord, I ask this in your name. Amen.
Prayers for Teenagers

48 Loving Creator,
thank you for this moment
when I feel your presence,
feel your hand
guiding my actions and my planning,
making me ready for new opportunities and new tasks.
Thank you for your presence with me.
Rosemary Atkins et al.

49 My Lord God, I have no idea where I am going. I do not see the road ahead of me. I cannot know for certain where it will end. Nor do I really know myself, and the fact that I think that I am following your will does not mean that I am actually doing so. But I believe that the desire to please you does in fact please you. And I hope I have that

desire in all that I am doing. I hope that I will never do anything apart from that desire. And I know that as I do this you will lead me by the right road, though I may know nothing about it. Therefore will I trust you always, though I may seem to be lost and in the shadow of death. I will not fear, for you are ever with me, and you will never leave me to face my perils alone.
Thomas Merton, 1915–68

50 O God, you created me and designed me for a purpose.
Help me to discern what that good and noble purpose is.
Let everything that is not the essential me fall away.
Amen.
Helen Jaeger

8

Saying thank you at the end of the day

———•◦•———

51 For the colours of the sky at the day's end, O God, and for
the quietness of night, I bring you my thanks:
> for birds homing through great spaces on confident
> wings; for wild creatures that seek shelter out of sight of
> human eyes; for little children gathered in safely and early
> to sleep; for all those weary and worn out who now enjoy
> the simple joys of family life.

Bless especially this night, O God, all far from home . . .
and all carrying on their work while others sleep: those
who have responsibility for planes, trains, ships, and cars;
those who minister to the sick, tend the mentally distressed,
restrain the reckless, or stand by those in sadness this night.
Amen.
Rita Snowden, 1907–99

52 I reverently speak in the presence of the Great Parent God:
I give Thee grateful thanks that Thou hast enabled me to
live this day, the whole day, in obedience to the excellent
spirit of Thy ways.
Japanese Shinto

53 I thank Thee, Father, for this another day that Thou hast
given me; for its joys and pleasures; for its gifts and graces;
for the food it has provided, and the friends it has brought

near; for the work I have been able to do, and for the periods
of rest; for the multitude of little things that make it big
with Thy mercy. Amen.
William Portsmouth

54 I turn now to grateful sleep,
   content to rest in Thy safekeeping.
   Amen.
   William Portsmouth

55 Lord, with your praise we drop off to sleep.
   Carry us through the night,
   make us fresh for the morning.
   Hallelujah for the day!
   And blessing for the night!
   A Ghanaian fisherman's prayer

56 O God, I thank you for life and being, and for all the
   blessings of the past day; for the love I have received
   and given, for all the kindnesses that I have received from
   others, for thy grace going before me and following after
   me. Above all I thank thee for him through whom I know
   thy love and receive thy grace, even Jesus Christ, my Lord
   and Saviour.
   George Appleton, 1902–93

57 O God, Who, by making the evening to succeed the day,
   hast bestowed the gift of repose on human weakness, grant,
   we beseech Thee, that while we enjoy those timely blessings
   we may acknowledge Him from Whom they come, even
   Jesus Christ our Lord. Amen.
   Mozarabic Liturgy

58 O Jesu Christ, thou joyous light of the holy glory of the
   Father, deathless, celestial, hallowed, blest: as we come to

the setting of the sun and behold the light of evening, we hymn thee, Father, Son, and Holy Spirit of God. Worthy art thou at all times to be hymned with hallowed voices, Son of God, who givest life; therefore praise from the whole world is thine.

Greek Vesper Hymn

9

Keeping short accounts with God

—•■•—

59 Grant, O Lord, that each day before I enter the little death of sleep, I may undergo the little judgement of the past day, so that every wrong deed may be forgiven and every unholy thought set right. Let nothing go down into the depths of my being which has not been forgiven and sanctified. Then I shall be ready for my final birth into eternity and look forward with hope and love to standing before thee, who art both judge and Saviour, holy judge and loving Saviour.
George Appleton, 1902–93

60 Lord, another day of my life has gone and I know that I have not used it as I could have done.

I have been selfish, tactless, thoughtless and unkind.

I have wanted too much for myself and forgotten my friends.

I have talked and talked, but I have not listened.

I have not listened to other people and now I do not know about their troubles and I cannot help them.

I have not listened, and therefore I cannot understand.

I have not stopped once all day, just to be quiet and listen to you either, Lord.

Lord, tomorrow you are going to give me another day.

Help me to use it better.

Tomorrow, Lord, help me to be quiet.
Virginia Salmon

61 Lord, we need you;
   our hearts are wounded,
   our days fade like evening shadows,
   we are weak and despise ourselves;
   for we have sinned against you:
   forgive us, O Lord,
   and in your constant love save us;
   through Jesus our redeemer. Amen.
   Michael Perry, from Psalm 109

62 Now evening has come, dear God. So many things have happened and the page of my book is full. I hope your eyes of love will find some beauty in it, and please forgive the blots and smudges.
   Phyllis Lovelock

63 O God, at the end of the day it is not so much the things that I have done which worry me as the things which I have not done.
   Forgive me for the tasks into which I did not put my best, for work that was shoddy, and for workmanship of which any true craftsman would be ashamed.
   Forgive me for the things I did not do, and for the help I did not give.
   Forgive me for the word of praise and the word of thanks I did not speak.
   Forgive me for my failure in courtesy and in graciousness to those with whom I live and work.
   Help me each day to do better, so that each night I may have fewer regrets: through Jesus Christ my Lord. Amen.
   William Barclay, 1907–78

64 O Lord, be gracious unto us! In all that we hear or see, in all that we say or do, be gracious unto us.
   I ask pardon of the Great God. I ask pardon at the sunset, when every sinner turns to Him. Now and for ever I ask

pardon of God. O Lord, cover us from our sins, guard our children, and protect our weaker friends.
Bedouin camel-driver's prayer

65 Penetrate the dark corners where we hide memories, and tendencies on which we do not care to look, but which we will not disinter and yield freely up to you, that you may purify and transmute them. The persistent buried grudge, the half-acknowledged enmity which is still smouldering; the bitterness of that loss we have not turned into sacrifice, the private comfort we cling to, the secret fear of failure which saps our initiative and is really inverted pride; the pessimism which is an insult to your joy. Lord, we bring all these to you, and we review them with shame and penitence in your steadfast light.
Evelyn Underhill, 1875–1941

66 The day fails; the darkness falls.
Now, O Lord my God,
now let thy servant lay him down in peace;
    for it is thou, Lord, only
        that makest him dwell in safety.

Out of mine own night let me call, let me cry,
    that I sleep not in sin unrepented.
Let my hands be clean,
    let my prayer be pure;
    let me look up to the brightness of thy glory,
        with whom is no darkness at all.
Let my lying down be very trust,
    mine eyes close under thy blessing.
Let action sleep, and memory, and even thought;
    but not love, never my hope in thee.
Into thy hands, O Lord,
    I commend my spirit.

While the body rests,
   quiet in thy keeping,
let my soul ascend
   and sing in thy light:
Hosanna in the highest.
Eric Milner-White, 1884–1963

67 The sun has gone to rest.
The bee forsakes the flowers.
The young bird slumbers in its nest,
within the leafy bowers.
Where have I been this day?
Into what folly run?
Forgive me, Father, when I pray,
through Jesus Christ thy Son.
Prayer on a sampler, 1857

10

When you're feeling lonely

---

68 Almighty God, remind us that nights of sorrow can be
followed by unexpected days of joy, and save us from the
sin of continuing self-pity. Amen.
Beryl Bye

69 Christ,
    praying in the Garden while others slept
    you know the necessity
    and the pain
    of standing alone.
    Be with me now in my loneliness.
    Help me to find strength in solitariness,
    peace in the silence,
    and the presence of God
    in the absence of friends.
    Turn my thoughts from myself
    that I may seek
    not so much to find companionship
    as to give companionship to others.
Margaret T. Taylor

70 Here I stand, O my God, alone.
    Have you forgotten me?
    I feel so far away from you, from other people, from the
world.
    I am alone.

How did I get here, in this lonely place? When did I lose that sense of your presence near me?

Who moved?

I try to tell myself that this is just a bad patch, that I'm tired, that too many things are going on in my life, that everything will be as it was –

if I just hang in there.

But I'm tired of just hanging in there and hoping that you and I will connect. I don't like feeling disjointed, uneasy, empty.

I am alone.

Where are you, God? How do I find you again? Where do I have to go? What do I have to do? I don't have any answers, and I can't hear your voice in my loneliness.

I long for the way it used to be: when I could feel your touch, your presence near me. How did I get lost?

Perhaps this is one of those times I will just have to walk in faith. God, here are three things I know:

- that you love me,
- that you have a plan for me,
- and that you are with me.

Even though I know those things, I don't *feel* them. If I did, I wouldn't be here now, telling you that I feel alone.

But I know those things because in the past, they were absolutely true. Just because I can't feel them now doesn't mean they're no longer true.

So, God, I'm going to begin a faith walk with you. I will believe that those three things are still true:

- that you love me,
- that you have a plan for me,
- and that you are with me.

32

Even if I feel alone.
    I offer you my faith walk. Please be with me, encourage and strengthen me, so that one day, maybe soon, I won't feel alone any more.
Patricia Wilson

71 Jesus, our brother,
    once you knelt sleepless
    in the darkness of a garden alone
    and wept and prayed,
    sweating, bleeding,
    with the pain of powerlessness,
    with the strain of waiting.
    An angel offered you strength –
    but it was a bitter cup.

    We pray for all
    who wake tonight
    waiting, agonizing,
    anxious and afraid,
    while others sleep:
    for those who sweat
    and bleed, and weep alone.

    If it is not possible
    for their cup to be taken away –
    then may they know your presence
    kneeling at their side.
    Jan Sutch Pickard

72 Lord, I'm lonely and I don't know who to turn to. I ask you to be with me, and with all people who are alone. To be alone is terrifying and everyone needs love. Comfort us, Lord God, for Jesus' sake. Amen.
    Prayers for Teenagers

73 Lord, I turn to You as my source of strength when I feel so
alone. I think of Christ and know that the loneliness He
felt in Gethsemane and on the cross must have been far
greater than I feel now. Still I find my feelings difficult to
bear. Thank You for being so accessible and understanding.
Help me to overcome my isolation and to reach out to
others again. In Christ's name, Amen.
Dr Jim Lewis

74 O God, I come to you for comfort.
You know how lonely I am, O God,
keep me from living too much in the past.
Keep me from living too much in memories and too
    little with hopes.
Keep me from being too sorry for myself.
Help me to remember that I am going through what
    many another has gone through.
Help me not to sorrow as those who have no hope.
Help me to find comfort in my work,
and, because I have gone through sorrow myself,
help me to help others who are in trouble.
This I ask for your love's sake. Amen.
The Seafarers' Prayer Book

75 The paths of lives criss-cross all around:
my neighbours busy with families and
tracking backwards and forwards to work.
Their time in the evenings is precious and pre-planned.

And here am I, Lord, in the middle of this
    thoroughfare:
a car passes, a dog barks or a postman makes
    impersonal deliveries.
When I get to the telephone, it's rarely anyone who
    knows me.

But it's good to talk, Lord,
for I am reminded that you, my dearest Friend, are
    always there,
have always known me, and understand my funny ways.
I smile, remembering the conversations we've had over
    the years.
Tomorrow, I'll tread my path again for the friendship and
    joy I hope to find.
Janet Gleadall

11

When you can't sleep

76 Good Jesus, strength of the weary, rest of the restless, by the weariness and unrest of your sacred cross, come to me who am weary, that I may rest in you.
E. B. Pusey, 1800–82

77 Lord Jesus, grant us Thy peace in sleepless hours, that in patience we may endure and in faith receive Thy strength to bring us victory. Amen.
Leslie F. Church

78 Loving God, You guard and protect all Your beloved children. Be with me now as I try to sleep. Let me feel safe, secure, and sleepy as I imagine myself resting in Your arms. Guide me into rest, that I may begin tomorrow afresh, to the glory of Your name. Amen.
Melissa Roberts

79 O Holy Spirit, bless all who have sleepless nights, and grant them patience, and fill their hearts with peace, for Jesus' sake. Amen.
S. B. Macey, nineteenth century

80 O Lord let me sleep! You have said that you will give your beloved sleep. I know you love me, please give me sleep. Or let me rest quietly in you and realize that I am sharing with you the sleeplessness of the starving, the lonely, the lost and

the old who are so much worse off than I. Let me know that my wakefulness is not wasted, but helps to make up what is lacking in your suffering.
Etta Gullick

81 O Lord, the Maker of all things, we pray Thee now in this evening hour, to defend us through thy mercy from all deceit of our enemy. Let us not be deluded with dreams, but if we lie awake keep thou our hearts. Grant this petition, O Father, to Whom with the Holy Ghost, always in heaven and earth, be all laud, praise and honour. Amen.
Henry VIII, 1491–1547

82 You, who said, 'Come unto me all ye who are weary and heavy-laden and I will give you rest', I come to you now.
   For I am weary indeed. Mentally and physically I am bone-tired. I am all wound up, locked up tight with tension. I am too tired to eat. Too tired to think. Too tired even to sleep. I feel close to the point of exhaustion.
   Lord, let your healing love flow through me.
   I can feel it easing my tensions. Thank you. I can feel my body relaxing. Thank you. I can feel my mind begin to go calm and quiet and composed.
   Thank you for unwinding me, Lord, for unlocking me. I am no longer tight and frozen with tiredness, but flowing freely, softly, gently into your healing rest.
Marjorie Holmes

12

Prayers for protection

——•◦•——

83 All that I love
      into Your keeping.
    All that I care for
      into your care.
    Be with us by day,
      be with us by night;
    and as dark closes
      the eyelids with sleep
    may I waken
      to the peace of a new day.
    Northumbria Community

84 Be present, O merciful God, and protect us through the silent
    hours of the night, that we who are wearied by the changes
    and chances of this fleeting world may repose upon thy eternal
    changelessness, through the everlasting Christ our Lord.
    Gelasian Sacramentary, AD 494

85 Come, Lord,
      and cover me with the night.
    Spread your grace over us
    as you assured us you would do.

    Your promises are more
    than all the stars in the sky;
    your mercy is deeper than the night.

38

Lord, it will be cold.
The night comes with its breath of death.
Night comes; the end comes; you come.
Lord, we wait for you
day and night.
African prayer

86 Dhe, teasruig an tigh, an teine, 's an tan.
Gach aon ta gabhail tamh an seo an nochd.
Teasruig mi fein 's mo chroilean graidh,
is gleidh sinn bho lamh 's bho lochd;
gleidh sinn bho namh an nochd,
air sgath Mhic Mhuire Mhathar
's an ait-s's gach ait a bheil an tamh an nochd,
air an oidhche nochd 's gach aon oidhche,
    an oidhche nochd 's gach aon oidhche.

God shield the house, the fire, the cattle,
every one who takes rest here tonight.
Shield myself and my beloved wee fold of children,
preserve us from violence and from harm;
preserve us from foes this night,
for the sake of the Son of the Mary Mother,
in this place, and in every place wherein they
    dwell tonight,
on this night and on every night,
    this night and every night.
Scottish Gaelic (translation adapted by
Anna Rogalski)

87 From ghoulies and ghosties
and long-leggedy beasties,
and things that go bump in the night,
good Lord, deliver us.
Traditional

88 I am placing my soul and my body
    in Thy safe keeping this night, O God,
    in Thy safe keeping, O Jesus Christ,
    in Thy safe keeping, O Spirit of Perfect Truth.
    The Three who would defend my cause
    be keeping me this night from harm.
    Northumbria Community

89 Lighten our darkness, we beseech thee, O Lord, and by thy
    great mercy defend us from all perils and dangers of this
    night; for the love of thy only Son, our Saviour Jesus Christ.
    Amen.
    Book of Common Prayer 1662

90 May the Almighty God take me, my family, my relations,
    my friends, my benefactors, and my enemies, under his
    gracious protection; give his holy angels charge concerning
    us; preserve us from the prince and powers of darkness,
    and from the dangers of the night; and keep us in perpetual
    peace and safety; through Jesus Christ our Lord.
    Thomas Wilson, 1663–1755

91 Now that we are going to lay ourselves down to sleep,
    take us into thy gracious protection,
    and settle our spirits in such quiet and delightful
        thoughts of the glory where our Lord Jesus lives,
    that we may desire to be dissolved and to go to him who
        died for us,
    that, whether we wake or sleep, we might live together
        with him.
    John Wesley, 1703–91

92 O heavenly Father, protect and bless all things that have breath:
    guard them from all evil and let them sleep in peace.
    Albert Schweitzer (when a child), 1875–1965

93 O Jesus, keep me in your sight,
   and guard me through the coming night.
   Sixth-century hymn

94 Preserve me, Lord, while I am waking, and defend me while
   I am sleeping, that my soul may continually watch for thee,
   and both body and soul may rest in thy peace for ever.
   John Cosin, 1594–1672

13

Night vigils

———◆———

95 Dear Lord, sometimes we find family responsibility more than we can bear. In those moments, strengthen us. Help us to help each other, that our burden may turn to joy.
Katharine Short

96 God be with the parents of all newborn babies, but especially those whose sleep will be broken once again tonight.

    Above all things, grant them the patience they need to bear the crying of their children.

    May their love for each other and the child of that love carry them through these trying days and nights. May it be as certain as the dawn.

    And in the meantime, ease the pain and hunger of their child so that they might know the magical, restoring power of sleep.
Kairos

97 He/she has not come home yet
    and I'm worried!
He/she always lets me know where he/she is.
My imagination is beginning to run riot!
Dear God,
    help me to stay calm.
    There will be a reasonable explanation.

If I need to do something, help me to act wisely.
I entrust him/her and all my family to you.
Lord, I trust you;
 strengthen my trust.
Rosemary Atkins et al. (adapted)

98 I commend to Thy mercy all who are awake this night:
 doctors tending the sick;
 nurses ministering to their wants;
 police and firemen guarding us;
 night-watchmen and those who drive on road and rail;
 men working on the sea, in the sky, and struggling
  with wind and wave;
 those who toss and turn in pain or restlessness;
 and those who only watch and wait.

May they know and welcome Thy sustaining love, doing
what they must as work for Thee, and use them, Lord, in
Thy great design for all men's good. Amen.
William Portsmouth

99 I've been concerned for hours,
 it seems like hours,
  hours of fear,
  hours of helplessness,
  hours with my mind racing through all the worst
  happenings
   of where he/she might be,
   of what he/she might be doing,
   of whom he/she might be with.
I've listened to all those squealing tyres –
 is that a fire engine or an ambulance?
Why is he/she so inconsiderate?
Why can't he/she understand how I feel?
I'm not happy about some of his/her friends,
 or their friends!

God of peace,
God of understanding,
give me now your peace, your understanding.
He/she will never understand our concern
    if we do not talk about it.
        When we talk, remind me to listen.
Rosemary Atkins et al.

100 Lord, I know she's no longer a child.
    I accept that she has a right to her own life.
    I know that I probably did the very same when I was
        her age.
    But Lord, I do worry when it's getting late and she's
        still not home.
    Please Lord keep her safe and help her to appreciate
        that just one phone call, saying she'll be home late,
        would make a difference.
    Kairos

101 Lord, we give into your care our children who are caus-
    ing us so much worry. The days are gone when we could
    correct them and tell them what to do. Now that they are
    grown up we have to stand by and watch them making
    mistakes and doing what is foolish or wrong.

    Thank you that you have gone on loving and forgiving
    us, your wayward children, over many years. Help us to
    be loving and forgiving to our own children. Help us never
    to stop praying for them. We earnestly ask you to bring
    them back to yourself and to us.

    Ease our own torment and distress and give us peace
    in trusting you, especially in the dark hours of the night.
    You are our heavenly Father, who loves our children more
    than we do and we bring them to you now, in Jesus' name.
    Mary Batchelor

102 Loving God,
    be near us with your strength and your peace
    as we wait and watch with ——
    as he/she journeys from us to his/her eternity.
May he/she know our presence and our love
    until he/she comes into the radiancy of
        your presence
    and knows the certainty of your love for
        him/her.
Into your everlasting arms
    we commend our dear one.
Rosemary Atkins et al. (adapted)

103 Oh, Lord, I hear it again, that little voice in the night, crying, 'Mummy!'

At least I think I hear it. It may be my imagination. It may be just the wind. Or if not, maybe it will stop in a minute, the child will go back to sleep . . .

(Oh, let it be just the wind. Or let him go back to sleep. I'm so tired. I've been up so many nights lately. I've got to get some sleep too.)

But if it's true, if it's one of them needing me and it isn't going to stop, if I must go – help me.

Lift me up, steady me on my feet. And make me equal to my duty.

If he's scared give me patience and compassion to drive the fears of the night away.

If he's ill give me wisdom. Make me alert. Let me know what to do.

If he's wet the bed again, give me even more patience and wisdom and understanding (and let me find some clean sheets).

Thank you, Lord, for helping my weary footsteps along the landing.

Thank you for sustaining me too as I comfort and care for the child.

Thank you for my own sweet ... sweet ... eventual sleep.

Marjorie Holmes

14

For people who work at night

—◦•◦—

104 As darkness is drawn about me, and the stars come
out, let my trust in thee deepen. As the interests of the
day are recalled, let none that causes thee pain remain
unforgiven.

Support with thy secret gifts of strength and calm all
who minister to the aged and sick; and all who speed
others through the night, by plane, ship and train; and
all who go 'down to the sea in ships'. Give good judgement and considerateness to those who travel by road –
that our highways may serve the issues of life, and not
death.

Comfort those who find themselves in strange settings
this night – far from home, in hospital, among strangers.
And so keep us all – because in this life we cannot keep
ourselves, now or ever. Amen.
Rita Snowden, 1907–99

105 As the days grow longer, Lord, my thoughts turn to those
whose working day is done in darkness. When I'm settling
down to sleep, others will be starting work that will take
them through the night and into morning. The night
shift is a difficult one, the grey glare of fluorescents,
the loneliness and tiredness all take their toll. Lord,
bless all those who work tonight, the factory workers,
the gardaí, the fire and ambulance services. See them
safely through the long, silent hours of the night, and

when their work is finally finished, grant them a good day's rest.
Kairos

106 Bless, O Lord, we pray you, those who wake and work that we may sleep: the policeman and the fireman who protect us; those who look after people who are ill; those who work beneath the earth; those who serve our commerce by road, rail, sea and air, and those who carry our news to near or distant places.

Guard them as they guard and serve us, and watch over them in danger and loneliness, for the sake of him who prayed for us in the watches of the night, Jesus Christ, our Lord.
B. A. Leary

107 Lord of all our aches and pain
help us so to use the brain
thou gavest us, that we may share
the pain which others have to bear,
thus linking them to us and thee,
thyself the Watch . . .
Help us to be minutes of thy times.

Grant Lord that we may bless
the hours when we receive
rest from thy hands
and peaceful sleep.
We thank thee, Lord,
and vigil keep.
Lucy Smith

108 O God, Who never sleepest, and art never weary, have mercy upon those who watch to-night; on the sentry, that he may be alert; on those who command, that they may

be strengthened with counsel; on the sick, that they may obtain sleep; on the wounded, that they may find ease; on the faint-hearted, lest they forget Thee; on the dying, that they may find peace; on the sinful, that they may turn again. And save us, O good Lord. Amen.
William Charles Edmund Newbolt, 1844–1930

109 Our Father . . . we remember those who must wake that we may sleep: bless those who watch over us at night, the guardians of the peace, the watchers who save us from the terrors of fire, and all the many who carry on through the hours of the night, the restless commerce of men on land and sea. We thank thee for their faithfulness and sense of duty; we pray thee for thy pardon if our covetousness or luxury make their nightly toil necessary: grant that we may realize how dependent the safety of our loved ones and the comforts of life are on these our brothers and sisters, so that we may think of them with love and gratitude and help to make their burden lighter. Through Jesus Christ our Lord. Amen.
Anon.

110 Watch thou, dear Lord, with those who wake or watch or weep tonight, and give thine angels charge over those who sleep. Tend thy sick ones, O Lord Christ; rest thy weary ones. Bless thy dying ones. Soothe thy suffering ones. Pity thine afflicted ones. Shield thy joyous ones. And all for thy love's sake.
Augustine of Hippo, 354–430

111 We ask thee to bless those for whom there will be no sleep tonight; those who must work throughout the night; those who journey through the night by sea or land or air, to bring us our food, our letters, and our newspapers for the morning; those who must be on duty all night to maintain

the public services, and to ensure the safety and the security of others; doctors who must wake to usher new life into the world, to close the eyes of those for whom this life is passing away, to ease the sufferer's pain; nurses and all who watch by the bedside of those who are ill; those who this night will not sleep because of the pain of their body or the distress of their mind; those in misfortune, who will lie down in hunger and cold.

Grant that in our own happiness and our own comfort we may never forget the sorrow and the pain, the loneliness and the need of others in the slow, dark hours. This we ask for Thy love's sake. Amen.
William Barclay, 1907–78

112 You are the Lamp
who does not go out at night.
We pray for the night workers
who rise at crack of dawn,
who do night shifts,
who work long hours in hospitals,
factories, studios, fields,
taxis, trains, and homes.
Be their Lamp
who does not go out at night.
Jonny Baker

15

For a difficult day tomorrow

---

113 Dear Lord, as I kneel to make my daily supplication, I ask especially that you should be by my side tomorrow, to give me support and guidance in what promises to be a challenging time, when difficult decisions must be made. Like a new-planted tree, I need support against the winds of circumstance and you have never failed me yet. I have never felt so much in need of a friend: be my friend and mentor tomorrow.
Peter Rowlett

114 Father, thank You for all the blessings You have given us today (especially ——). Please take away worries about tomorrow, because we know You can deal with them when the time comes. Amen.
Beryl Bye

115 God, it's time to put away the books and notes. The first exam is in the morning and I do feel nervous.
　　What if I can't remember anything?
　　What if the questions are awful?
　　So much depends on those few hours in the exam hall.
　　Be with all of us who will find it difficult to sleep tonight.
　　Be with us as we begin our exams tomorrow and stay with us through the difficult days ahead.
Kairos

116 Lord, I ask to feel your presence with me tomorrow.
My mind is full of the possibilities and outcomes.
Painful choices may need to be made.
May I now lay all my thoughts and worries at your feet
and look up to you in trust
reassured that the weight and the hurt will be eased by
   your strength and love.
I ask that Your Will be done. Amen.
Janet Gleadall

117 O God, the source of all health, fill my heart with faith. Be near me in times of weakness and pain. Although I know you are in control, I am apprehensive about what faces me. You made me, loved me, and have provided my surgeon with needed skill to perform a miracle on my behalf. Sustain me by Your grace that my strength and courage may not fail; heal me according to Your will. Amen.
Dr Charles E. Frankum

118 O God, we start exams tomorrow. I've studied hard but I'm sure I haven't learned enough, and I cannot always remember what I've learned.
   Please help me to keep calm and not be worried, so that I'll remember what I've learned and do my best. Then, even if I fail I need not be ashamed, and if I pass, please help me not to boast, but give my thanks to you for helping me to use the gifts which you have given. Thank you, God.
Nancy Martin

16

The night as a time for intimacy and love

———◆———

119 Creator God,
    Creator of our lives,
    Creator of our love;
      today our words gave witness to the world
    of the love of our hearts and minds.
    Tonight our bodies give witness to each other
    of the passion and longing of that love.
      May we be
    sensitive to the needs of each other,
    learning how to delight and to caress.
      May we be
    strong in gentleness,
    tender in newness,
    patient in uncertainty,
    growing in understanding,
    caring always for our bodies
      for they are the temples of your Spirit.
    Rosemary Atkins et al.

120 Dear God, in your wisdom and generosity you have given
us two kinds of Love: Agape, the love we feel for you, our
Creator; and Eros, the earthly love we feel for our partner.
In this world, which can sometimes show us sorrow and
disappointment, human love can be a great comfort and

53

healer. Especially at night, in those dark hours of uncertainty, the act of human intimacy is a great gift, and later, a time when we can be close and talk together of our love, and finally, find peace in a sleep that heals and refreshes. Thank you, Lord.
Peter Rowlett

121 Jesus, in your earthly life
    you knew the necessity
        of times of quietness,
        of times of being away from the crowds.
   . . .
   Now we have time together – at last,
    time to share our love
      in the total giving
      of our bodies to each other;
    time to relax and to caress,
      to talk and to be silent;
    time to unwind from all the pressures,
    time to rejoice in the love you have given us.
Rosemary Atkins et al.

122 Oh, God, thank you for this beautiful hour of love.
   My dear is asleep now, but I am too filled with the wonder and joy of it to sleep just yet.
   I stand at the window gazing up at your star-riddled sky. I lean on the sill and gaze down upon your quiet earth.
   How rich and fruitful it smells, how fragrant with life and the promise of life.
   I see your trees reaching out as if to each other. For even trees must have mates to mature. Then they cast down their seeds and the rich fertile earth receives them to bear afresh.
   I see the glow-worms twinkling, hear the song of the nightingale and the hoot of the owl. All are calling, calling, insistently, 'Here I am! Come. Come to me!'

'Male and female created he them,' I think. For everything must have its opposite and meet with its opposite to be fulfilled.

Thank you, God, for this remarkable plan. Thank you for the hours of love it means.

I am as happy as one of those nightingales singing in the branches.

I feel as tall and strong and lovely as one of those out-reaching trees. I feel as complete yet filled with promise as the earth teeming with seeds.

Thank you, God, for making me a woman.
Marjorie Holmes

17

The healing aspect of sleep

123 Be the peace of the Spirit mine this night.
Be the peace of the Son mine this night.
Be the peace of the Father mine this night.
The peace of all peace be mine this night.
Northumbria Community

124 Deep and silent and cool as a broad, still,
     tree-shaded river
is the peace of thy presence, thou rest of our souls.
From the thousand problems of this our hurrying life
we turn, with silent joy, to plunge in thee,
to steep our souls in thy quiet depths
where no clamour of earth disturbs our perfect content.
Thou art our home and refuge;
in thee we are safe and at peace:
ever in the din and hurry of the world
we know that thou art near,
we know that close at hand – closer than our little life –
floweth that silent river of thy presence and love.
In a moment be surrounded and soaked in thy peace:
in a moment, as this loud world clangs round us,
we may rest secure in the bliss of thine eternity.
J. S. Hoyland, 1887–1957

125 In the night of weariness let me give myself up to sleep
without struggle, resting my trust upon thee. Let me not

force my flagging spirit into a poor preparation for thy worship. It is thou who drawest the veil of night upon the tired eyes of the day to renew its sight in a fresher gladness of awakening.
Rabindranath Tagore, 1861–1941

126 I've had a long soak in the bath with soothing bath stuff and I can feel the aches and pains seep out of me. And now it's time for bed. Oh how lovely, Lord: hours of gentle healing sleep! Bless me as I creep in under the covers. Bless me as I set my head on the pillow. Bless me and soothe the hurts of body and mind as I close my eyes and settle under the protection of your love and care. Thank you for sleep, loving Lord. Let me wake tomorrow restored and able to go on. Amen.
Dorothy M. Stewart

127 O Lord Jesus Christ, our watchman and keeper, take us to thy care: grant that, our bodies sleeping, our minds may watch in thee, and be made merry by some sight of that celestial and heavenly life, wherein thou art the King and Prince, together with the Father and the Holy Spirit, where the angels and holy souls be most happy citizens. O purify our souls, keep clean our bodies, that in both we may please thee, sleeping and waking, for ever.
Christian Prayers, 1566

128 This little one I hold is my child:
she is your child also,
therefore be gracious to her.
She has come into a world of trouble; sickness is in
    the world, and cold, and pain –
pain which you knew
and with which you were familiar.

Let her sleep peacefully,
for there is healing in sleep:
do not be angry with me or my child.
Let her grow: let her become strong:
let her become full-grown:
then she will worship you and delight your heart.
From the Aro people, Sierra Leone

18

God in the darkness

129 As the rain hides the stars,
      as the autumn mist hides the hills,
      as the clouds veil the blue of the sky,
      so the dark happenings of my lot
      hide the shining of Thy face from me.
      Yet, if I may hold Your hand in the darkness . . .
      it is enough,
      since I know that
      although I may stumble in my going,
      Thou dost not fall.
      Anon.

130 Heavenly Father, hear our voice out of our deep sorrow.
      We know that Thou art with us, and that whatsoever
      cometh is a revelation of Thine unchanging love. Thou
      knowest what is best for us. Thy will be done. O keep our
      souls from all the temptations of this hour of mourning,
      that we may neither sorrow as those without hope, nor
      lose our trust in Thee; but that the darker this earthly
      scene becometh the lighter may be our vision of that
      eternal world where all live before Thee; through Jesus
      Christ our Lord. Amen.
      Laurence Tuttiett, 1825–97 (adapted)

131 Lord, give us grace to hold to thee
      when all is weariness and fear

and sin abounds within, without,
when that I would do I cannot do
and that I do I would not do,
when love is tested by the doubt
that love is false or dead within the soul,
when every act brings new confusion, new distress,
new opportunities, new misunderstanding,
and every thought new accusation.
Lord give us grace
that we may know that in the darkness pressing
    round
it is the mist that hides thy face;
that thou art there
and thou dost know we love thee still.
Gilbert Shaw, 1886–1967

132 Lord,
    it is night.

The night is for stillness.
    Let us be still in the presence of God.
It is night after a long day.
    What has been done has been done;
    what has not been done has not been done;
    let it be.

The night is dark.
    Let our fears of the darkness of the world and of our
        own lives
    rest in you.

The night is quiet.
    Let the quietness of Your peace enfold us,
        all dear to us,
        and all who have no peace.

The night heralds the dawn.
   Let us look expectantly to a new day,
      new joys,
      new possibilities.

In your name we pray.
Amen.
John Williamson

133 Lord Jesus Christ,
   we have gathered for prayer as the day is
      nearly over.
   Though we cannot see you before us,
   enlighten the eyes of our hearts
   that we may recognise your presence
   and know that you are with us,
   and will stay beside us,
   this night and for ever more. Amen.
   Susan Durber

134 Lord, when it's dark and we can't feel your presence,
   and nothing seems real any more, and we're tempted to
   give up trying – help us to know that you are never really
   absent – that we are like a little child in its mother's arms,
   held so close to your heart that we cannot see your face,
   and that underneath are the everlasting arms.
   Margaret Dewey

135 My faith burns low, my hope burns low.
   Only my heart's desire cries out in me,
   by the deep thunder of its want and woe,
   cries out to Thee.

   Lord, Thou art Life tho' I be dead.
   Love's Fire thou art, however cold I be;

nor heaven have I, nor place to lay my head,
nor home, but Thee.
Christina Rossetti, 1830–94

136 We pray for those who find the night long and bleak,
for those who cry out for the morning,
that they may know the presence of God in the dark
   hours.
Susan Durber

19

Angels

---

137 As I lay down to sleep,
     may the guardian angel
     watch over me,
     coaxing all my cares
     to unravel into peace.

     As darkness within
     is wed to darkness without,
     freed from the weight of light,
     let my eyes sleep,
     relieved of all intensities.

     Let my imagination
     trawl the compressed seas
     to bless the dawn
     with a generous catch
     of luminous dream.

     May this new night of rest
     repair the wear of time
     and restore youth of heart
     for the adventure
     that awaits tomorrow.
     John O'Donohue

138 Good night, my Guardian Angel.
     The day has sped away.
     Well spent or ill, its story is written down for aye.
     And now by God's kind providence,
     thy image, pure and bright,
     watch over me while I'm sleeping.
     My Angel dear, good night.
     Irish childhood prayer

139 Lord, keep us safe this night,
     secure from all our fears.
     May Angels guard us while we sleep,
     till morning light appears.
     Amen.
     Traditional end of school-day prayer

140 O Christ, son of the living God,
     may Your holy angels guard our sleep,
     may they watch us as we rest
     and hover around our beds.

     Let them reveal to us in our dreams
     visions of Your glorious truth,
     O High Prince of the universe,
     O High Priest of the mysteries.

     May no dreams disturb our rest
     and no nightmares darken our dreams.
     May no fears or worries delay
     our willing, prompt repose.

     May the virtue of our daily work
     hallow our nightly prayers.
     May our sleep be deep and soft
     so our work will be fresh and hard.
     Northumbria Community

141 O Jesus, Du hast in Deiner Ölberg Verlassenheit und Todesangst um Trost zum himmlischen Vater gebetet.

Du weisst, es gibt Seelen, die auf Erden keine Stütze, keinen Tröster haben. Sende ihnen Engel, der ihnen Freude gibt!

O Jesus, in Thy great loneliness on the Mount of Olives, and in Thy agony, Thou didst pray to the Heavenly Father for comfort. Thou knowest that there are souls on earth who are without support and without comforters. Send them an angel to give them joy.
German prayer, trans. Barbara Greene

142 Sunk is the sun's last beam of light,
and now the world is wrapt in night,
Christ, light us with Thy heavenly ray,
nor let our feet in darkness stray.

Thanks, Lord, that Thou throughout
    the day
hast kept all grief and harm away;
that angels tarried round about
our coming in and going out.

Whate'er of wrong we've done or said,
let not the charge on us be laid;
that, through Thy free forgiveness blest,
in peaceful slumber we may rest.

Thy guardian angels round us place
all evil from our couch to chase;
our soul and body, while we sleep,
in safety, gracious Father, keep. Amen.
Nicolaus Herman, 1500–61,
trans. Frances Elizabeth Cox, 1841

143 Visit, O Lord, this dwelling, and drive far from it all the snares of the enemy; let thy holy angels dwell in it to preserve us in peace, and may thy blessing be upon us evermore; through Jesus Christ our Lord.
Office of Compline (adapted)

144 We give thanks unto thee, heavenly Father, through Jesus Christ, thy dear Son, that thou hast this day so graciously protected us, and we beseech thee to forgive us all our sins, and the wrong which we have done, and by thy great mercy defend us from all the perils and dangers of this night. Into thy hands we commend our bodies and souls, and all that is ours. Let thy holy angel have charge concerning us, that the wicked one have no power over us. Amen.
Martin Luther, 1483–1546

20

For sweet dreams

145 As my head rests on my pillow,
     let my soul rest in your mercy.

     As my limbs relax on my mattress,
     let my soul relax in your peace.

     As my body finds warmth beneath the blankets,
     let my soul find warmth in your love.

     As my mind is filled with dreams,
     let my soul be filled with visions of heaven.
     Johann Freylinghausen, 1670–1739

146 Before the ending of the day,
     Creator of the world we pray,
     that with Thy wonted favour thou
     wouldst be our guard and keeper now.

     From all ill dreams defend our eyes,
     from nightly fears and fantasies,
     tread under foot our ghostly foe,
     that no pollution we may know.

     O Father, that we ask be done,
     through Jesus Christ, thine only Son,
     Who with the Holy Ghost and thee,
     doth live and reign eternally.
     Ancient Compline hymn, trans. J. M. Neale, 1852

147 Father . . .
    keep us so close to Your heart
    that even our dreams are peaceful,
    and that we may see things . . .
    more and more from Your point of view.
    Corrie ten Boom, 1892–1983

148 God of all our Dreamtimes, we bring you our dreams.
    You dreamed a new dream in your Eden garden,
    lived through a shattered dream in your Gethsemane
        garden,
    experienced a fulfilled dream in your burial garden.
    Through the dreams of your people
    you have covenanted, warned, prepared, promised.
    Plant your strong Spirit of trust and hope
    in our dream gardens, we pray. Amen.
    Commission for Mission, Uniting Church in Australia

149 Lord Jesus Christ, you are the gentle moon and joyful stars, that watch over the darkest night. You are the source of all peace, reconciling the whole universe to the Father. You are the source of all rest, calming troubled hearts, and bringing sleep to weary bodies. You are the sweetness that fills our minds with quiet joy, and can turn the worst nightmares into dreams of heaven. May I dream of your sweetness, rest in your arms, be at one with your Father, and be comforted in the knowledge that you always watch over me.
    Erasmus, 1469–1536

150 Nurture us, gracious Lord, as we sleep peacefully
        through the night.
    Guard our souls and comfort our hearts.
    Gentle our busy minds and soothe away the stresses
        of the day.

Send sweet dreams that curve our sleeping lips in smiles
and wake us to fresh joy and eagerness.
Amen.
Dorothy M. Stewart

151 O God,
who through thy ordering of our inner nature
dost show us truths about ourselves as we sleep:
help us to interpret these messages
from the depths of our being,
and to know and accept ourselves
as the starting-point for growth
towards the pattern of thy Son,
Jesus Christ our Lord.
George Appleton, 1902–93

152 Sleep in peace.
Sleep soundly.
Sleep in love.
Weaver of dreams,
weave well in us as we sleep.
Ray Simpson

21

Approaching the end of life

153 Abide with us, O Lord, for it is toward evening and the
day is far spent; abide with us, and with thy whole Church.
Abide with us in the evening of the day, in the evening of
life, in the evening of the world. Abide with us in thy grace
and mercy, in holy Word and sacrament, in thy comfort and
thy blessing. Abide with us in the night of distress and fear,
in the night of doubt and temptation, in the night of bitter
death, when these shall overtake us. Abide with us and with
all thy faithful ones, O Lord, in time and in eternity.
Lutheran Manual of Prayer

154 As each day passes,
the end of my life becomes ever nearer,
and my sins increase in number.
You, Lord, my Creator, know how feeble I am,
and in my weakness, strengthen me;
when I suffer, uphold me,
and I will glorify you,
my Lord and my God.
Ephraem of Syria, 306–373

155 As the day closes, I know more surely than ever that in thee
I live and move and have my being. Thou hast set me to
live in this time and place – and I bring thee thanks for this
wonderful experience. Thou hast not meant me to walk alone,
but in the helpful fellowship of others I call 'my friends'.

Grant new understanding to all who find life difficult as the years go by and infirmities multiply. Deliver us from self-pity that blinds us to the needs of others about us, day by day. Come, when we are sad, to comfort us; when we are dull, to brighten us; when we are tired, to refresh our spirits.

All my loved ones I commend to thee, knowing full well that they were loved of thee, before ever I loved them.

Gather us in – we are all thy children.

Amen.

Rita Snowden, 1907–99

156 Having passed over this day, Lord, I give thanks
    unto thee.
The evening draweth nigh, make it comfortable.
An evening there is, as of the day, so of this life.
The evening of this life of old-age,
Old-age hath seiz'd upon me; make that comfortable.
Cast me not away in the time of age;
Forsake me not when my strength faileth me. (Psalm 71.9)
Be thou with me until old-age and even to hoar hairs
    do thou carrie me. (Isaiah 46.4)
Do thou do it, do thou forgive, do thou receive and save
    me, O Lord.
Tarrie thou with me, O Lord, for it is toward evening
    with me and the day is far spent (Luke 24.29) of this
    my toilsome life.
Let thy strength be made perfect in my weakness.
    (2 Corinthians 12.9)

Lancelot Andrewes, 1555–1626

157 Lord,
grant that my last hour
may be my best hour.

John Aubrey, 1626–97

158 Lord, I am coming as fast as I can.
   I know I must pass through the shadow of death before
      I can come to see thee,
   but it is but a mere shadow of death, a little darkness
      upon nature;
   but thou by thy merits and passion hast broke through
      the jaws of death.
   So, Lord, receive my soul, and have mercy upon me.
   William Laud, 1573–1645

159 Lord, you have taken the fear of death away from us. The
   end of our life here you have made the beginning of the
   true life . . .
      To free us from sin and from the curse laid upon us,
   you took both sin and the curse upon yourself . . .
      When you shattered the gates of hell and trampled
   the Devil, death's lord, you cleared the way for our
   resurrection.
      Set now an angel of light beside me and bid him take
   my hand and lead me to the resting-place where there is
   water for refreshment . . .
      If out of weakness of human nature I have fallen and
   sinned in word or deed or thought, forgive it me; for you
   have power to forgive sins on earth. When I am divested
   of my body, may I stand before you with my soul unspotted:
   receive it, blameless and faultless, with your own hands.
   Macrina the Younger, c.327–379

160 O Lord our God,
   under the shadow of your wings we will rest.
   Defend us and support us,
   bear us up when we are little,
   and we know that even down to our grey hairs,
   you will carry us.
   Augustine of Hippo, 354–430

161 Sometimes, O Lord, as I look back, my youth and young
adulthood seem far off. But in reality, I know they are but
a moment in the memory of nations. So many changes
have come, so many habits and standards now are new.
It is difficult at times to have patience with the makers of
today. At the heart of things, I am glad of thine unchanging
character – what Jesus was in time, thou art eternally.
He said so! And he encouraged us reverently to call thee
'Father'. This is a wonderful reality – and it involves the
brotherhood and sisterhood of mankind, thy children.
I am sorry for some foolishnesses today – help me to mend
them. And send me to sleep forgiven – and so at peace.
Amen.
Rita Snowden, 1907–99

22

Bedtime prayers for children and young people

162 Dear God, another day has passed.
　　 Another night has come at last.
　　 Your watchful tender love will keep
　　 me guarded safely while I sleep.
　　 The quiet night is soft and kind.
　　 It rests my body, heart, and mind.
　　 The dreams that come are sure to be
　　 God's night-time messages to me.
　　 I'll sleep and rest the whole night long,
　　 that I may grow both big and strong.
　　 God bless and keep my dear ones, then
　　 God bless everybody else. Amen.
　　 Anon.

163 Good night!
　　 May the Great Father of us all
　　 hold us in His keeping,
　　 and guard us all this night
　　 till dawn of day.
　　 Good night!
　　 Girl Guides

164 Gud, som haver barnen kär,
　　 se till mig som liten är.

Vart jag mig i världen vänder,
star min lycka i Guds hander.
Lyckan kommer, lycken går,
du förbliver Fader vår.

Lord, who loves children,
watch over me, who is small.
When I wander in the world,
my fortune is kept in God's hands.
Happiness comes, happiness goes,
but you will always be our Father.
Swedish prayer, 1780

165 Jesus, tender Shepherd, hear me;
bless Thy little lamb tonight;
through the darkness be Thou near me;
watch my sleep till morning light.

All this day Thy hand has led me,
and I thank Thee for Thy care;
Thou hast warmed and clothed and
    fed me;
listen to my evening prayer.
Mary L. Duncan, 1814–40

166 Matthew, Mark, Luke and John,
bless the bed which I lie on.
Four corners have I to my bed;
at them four angels nightly spread.
One to watch and one to pray
and one to bear my soul away.
Traditional

167 O God, unseen but ever near,
keep me this night from every fear,

75

and when shall come another day,
and I begin once more my work and play,
may I be good and kind and true,
and do the things I ought to do.
Anon.

168 O Jesus, Gracious Saviour,
   tonight I come to thee.
   Oh may thy gracious favour
   rest on a child like me.
   And now, O Lord, I ask thee
   to bless me as I sleep.
   Throughout the hours of darkness
   thy child in safety keep.
   Sunday School prayer

169 O Lord Jesus Christ, who didst receive the children who
   came to Thee, receive also from me, Thy child, this evening
   prayer. Shelter me under the shadow of Thy wings, that
   in peace I may lie down and sleep; and do Thou waken
   me in due time, that I may glorify Thee, for Thou alone
   art righteous and merciful. Amen.
   Eastern Church

170 Rhof fy mhen i lawr i gysgu,
   rhof fy ngofal i Grist Iesu;
   os byddaf farw cyn y bore,
   Duw dderbynio f'enaid inne.

   Now I lay me down to sleep,
   I pray the Lord my soul to keep.
   If I should die before I wake
   I pray the Lord my soul to take.
   Welsh traditional

171 The good of today I thank you for,
   the bad of today I am sorry for,
   the world of today I pray for.
   Lord, I am trying to trust you and love you.
   I trust myself to you tonight.
   Young Christians at Prayer

172 When I'm put to bed today,
   both my eyes I'll shut and say:
   Father, till the morning light,
   watch my little bed tonight.

   All the people in all lands
   take into thy loving hands.
   Old and young and great and small,
   from all dangers guard them all.

   Give the sick ones gentle sleep.
   Dry the eyes of those that weep.
   And please leave the moon to light
   all poor travellers through the night.
   Borthyn County Primary School, Ruthin,
   North Wales, 1923

23

Christmas, New Year, Easter, Sundays: special times and seasons

———◆◆◆———

173 O Great God of the night and of the day, praise be unto thee:

praise be unto thee for this the long night of flake and drift, of white snow until the day, of a white moon until the dawn;

for this night is the eve of the great birth when the Son was born to the Virgin Mary, Jesus thy son, O King of glory, who is the stock of our joy;

for this night when the sun edged the high hills with light, when sea and land were edged with light, when Christ the King of greatness was born;

before the sound of the glory coming was known, the sound of the wave was on the strand, before the sound of his footfall upon the ground was known, the sound of the song of the glorious angels rang forth on this long night;

wood and tree were shining, hill and water, field and vale were shining when his step came to the earth; all praise be unto thee.

Amen.

Traditional Gaelic, trans. G. R. D. McLean

174 O God, our Father, we thank Thee for the happiness of
this Christmas Day . . .

 Now at evening time we specially remember those
for whom Christmas has not been a happy time. Bless
those to whom sorrow came, and for whom it was all
the sorer, because it came at the time when everyone
else was so happy. Bless those who have no friends, no
homes, no family circle, no one to remember them;
and be with them in their loneliness to comfort and
to cheer them . . . Through Jesus Christ our Lord.
Amen.
William Barclay, 1907–78

175 Grant, Lord, that as the years change we may find rest
in your eternal changelessness. May we go forward into
this year with courage, sure in the faith that while life
changes around us, you are always the same, guiding
us with your wisdom and protecting us with your love.
So may the peace which passes understanding keep our
hearts and minds in Christ Jesus, and your blessing be
upon all nations and upon all whom we love, in the name
of the Father, and of the Son, and of the Holy Spirit.
Amen.
Harold E. Evans

176 Look upon us tonight, Lord, as we pray to you, with
our tiny resolutions and enormous fears; our tiny
achievements and enormous failings; our tiny vision
and enormous tasks. Be with those who are very con-
scious of the vanity and frustration of the world,
and show them that Christ makes all things new. Be
with those also who do not feel this frustration; be
with the self-satisfied, the rich, the proud and the power-
ful, that they may see in Christ a much more excellent
way.

Look upon our homes and families and dear ones; those from whom we are separated, those for whom we are anxious, those with whom we have quarrelled. Bring into every human relationship the unity and healing and strength of your Son.

Look upon our church in all its needs. Come among us in refreshing and reviving power in this coming year.

Look upon our world with all its waste and war and sorrow, and all its joys as well; and make your believing people more effective in serving it, in bringing it light, and in sharing with it the fragrance of Christ.

All these things we ask for the honour of his name.
Christopher Idle

177 O God, our Father, tonight we are looking back across the year which is passing from us now.

There is so much for which we need forgiveness.

For the time we have wasted; for the opportunities we have neglected; for the strength we have given to the wrong things; for all the mistakes we have made:

forgive us, O God.

There is so much for which we ought to give Thee thanks. For health and strength; for protection in the time of danger; for healing in the time of illness; for upholding in the day of sorrow; for daily light and daily leading:

we thank Thee, O God.

Bless those for whom this has been a happy year, and make them to give the thanks to Thee. Bless those for whom this has been a sad year, and help them still to face the future with steady eyes. And help us in the

year to come so to live that at the end of it we shall
also not only be one year older, but that we shall also be
one year nearer Thee. This we ask for Thy love's sake.
Amen.
William Barclay, 1907–78

178 Lord, it is hard to concentrate our thoughts for very
long on what happened nearly two thousand years
ago. Somehow the cross on the hill seems so remote ...
Yet the sins of those who crucified Jesus are our sins.
Our needs are the needs of all mankind. Help us tonight
to see the cross, eternal not only in the heart of God but
in the hearts of us men and women. So may we receive
your forgiveness and your peace, through Jesus Christ our
Lord. Amen.
J. D. Searle

179 We would now dismiss the cares of the world with the
week. May we rise in the morning with refreshed bodies
and renewed strength, and be in the Spirit on the Lord's
Day. And do thou send out Thy Light and Thy Truth, that
they may lead us and guide us, to Thy holy hill and to
thyself; through Jesus Christ our Lord. Amen.
Fielding Ould, 1864

180 O Lord of our life, Who hast given us the rest of this
sacred day, grant that the benediction of its restfulness
may abide upon us throughout the week. Enable us to
carry the influence of its consecration into all that we do;
let the praises of our lips rendered to thee this day become
praise in our lives. May the power of thy love be with us
in every duty, that by pureness, by knowledge, and by
tenderness we may glorify Thee; through Jesus Christ.
Amen.
William Boyd Carpenter, 1841–1918

181 Short days, sharp days, long nights come on apace,
   ah, who shall hide us from the winter's face?
   Cold doth increase, the sickness will not cease,
   and here we lie, God knows, with little ease.
   From winter, plague, and pestilence, good Lord, deliver us!
   Thomas Nashe, 1567–1601

24

The unsleeping Church

———◆·●·◆———

182 As the darkness falls and the shadows grow . . .
Come, Lord Jesus.
When we are tired and weary and longing for rest . . .
Come, Lord Jesus.
While the business of the world goes on and when there
   is no silence . . .
Come, Lord Jesus.
Whenever we meet together to curse the darkness and
   to light a flame for justice . . .
Come, Lord Jesus.
While we cannot find your peace in the world and long
   for your blessing . . .
Come, Lord Jesus.
As we join in the great circle of prayer with all your saints . . .
Come, Lord Jesus. Amen.
Susan Durber

183 The day thou gavest, Lord, is ended,
the darkness falls at thy behest;
to thee our morning hymns ascended,
thy praise shall sanctify our rest.

We thank thee that thy church unsleeping,
while earth rolls onward into light,
through all the world her watch is keeping,
and rests not now by day or night.

As o'er each continent and island
the dawn leads on another day,
the voice of prayer is never silent,
nor dies the strain of praise away.

The sun that bids us rest is waking
our brethren 'neath the western sky,
and hour by hour fresh lips are making
thy wondrous doings heard on high.

So be it, Lord; thy throne shall never,
like earth's proud empires, pass away;
thy kingdom stands, and grows for ever,
till all thy creatures own thy sway.
John Ellerton, 1826–93

Acknowledgements

———◆●◆———

The compiler and publisher are pleased to acknowledge the authors and publishers of the works listed below for permission to quote from their copyrighted material. Every effort has been made to track all sources and copyright holders. The compiler and publisher apologize for any errors or omissions and, if notified, will rectify them at the earliest opportunity. Special thanks are due to those authors whose work is being published here for the first time. Numbers refer to the prayer numbers.

Alcuin: 4 from *Prayers for this Life*, ed. Christopher Howse (London: Continuum, 2005).

George Appleton: 56 and 151 from *One Man's Prayers* by George Appleton (London: SPCK, 1977), by permission of SPCK; 40 and 59 from *Journey for a Soul* (London: Collins Fontana, 1974).

Rosemary Atkins et al.: 12, 15, 48, 97, 99, 102, 119, 121 from *Joined in Love* by Rosemary Atkins, Dorothy Brooker, Rosalind Buddo, Philippa Chambers, Audrey England and Alice White (London: Collins, 1988).

Jonny Baker: 36, 112 from *Quiet Spaces: Night*, BRF (<www.brf.org.uk>), 2008, used by permission.

William Barclay: 32, 111, 174, 177 from *The Plain Man's Book of Prayers* by William Barclay (London: Fount, 1959); 6, 39, 63 from *More Prayers for the Plain Man* by William Barclay (London: Fontana, 1962). By kind permission of the Trustee and Executor, Donald W. F. Currie at Alexander McAllister & McKechnie, Paisley.

Mary Batchelor: 101 taken from *Women of Prayer* by Dorothy M. Stewart, published by Lion Hudson plc, 1993. Copyright © 1993 Mary Batchelor (deceased). Used with permission of Lion Hudson plc.

The Book of Common Prayer: Extracts from The Book of Common Prayer, the rights in which are vested in the Crown, are reproduced by permission of the Crown's Patentee, Cambridge University Press.

Borthyn County Primary School: 172 by kind permission of Borthyn Controlled Primary School, Denbighshire, Wales.

Ian Bunting: 22 from *Prayers for Today's Church*, ed. Dick Williams (London: Falcon Books/CPAS, 1972), with permission, <www.cpas.org.uk>.

Beryl Bye: 68, 114 from *Hear a Minute* by Beryl Bye, © Lutterworth Press, 1990.

Amy Carmichael: 24 from *Rose from Brier* by Amy Carmichael, © 1933 by the Dohnavur Fellowship; 41 from *Gold Cord* by Amy Carmichael, © 1991 by the Dohnavur Fellowship. Both prayers used by permission of CLC Publications. May not be further reproduced. All rights reserved.

Rex Chapman: 3 from *A Kind of Praying* by Rex Chapman, © SCM Press, 1970. Used by permission of Hymns Ancient & Modern Ltd.

Leslie F. Church: 77 from *Brave Heart: A Little Book for those who Suffer* by Leslie F. Church, Epworth Press © TMCP. Used by permission of the Methodist Church.

Commission for Mission of the Uniting Church in Australia: 148 from *Dare to Dream*, ed. Geoffrey Duncan (London: Fount, 1995) by permission of the Uniting Church in Australia.

Jean Crowther: 13 from *Oh God . . . 120 Celebrities' Prayers*, ed. Steve Chalke (Oxford: Lion, 1998), by kind permission of Steve Chalke, <www.oasisuk.org>.

Margaret Dewey: 134 from *Prayer is My Life* by Margaret Dewey (London: USPG, 1966), by permission of USPG: Anglicans in World Mission.

Susan Durber: 133, 136, 182 from *Worship – From the United Reformed Church* by the Doctrine, Worship and Prayer Committee, published by the United Reformed Church 2003, and used with permission.

Harold E. Evans: 175 from *Prayers for Today's Church*, ed. Dick Williams (London: Falcon Books/CPAS, 1972) with permission, <www.cpas.org.uk>.

Dr Charles E. Frankum: 117 from the Baptist Memorial Hospital Chaplaincy Centre website.

Janet Gleadall: 9, 75, 116.

Barbara Greene: 141 from *God of a Hundred Names*, comp. and ed. Barbara Greene and Victor Gollancz (London: Victor Gollancz, 1962).

Etta Gullick: 27, 80 from *The One Who Listens*, ed. Michael Hollings and Etta Gullick, published by McCrimmons, Great Wakering, Essex, 1971. Used with permission.

Giles Harcourt: 38 from *Short Prayers for the Long Day*, comp. Giles and Melville Harcourt (London: Collins, 1978).

Heather Harvey: 14 taken from *Give Me A Hand, Lord* by Heather Harvey, published and copyright © 1986 by Darton Longman and Todd Ltd, London, and used by permission of the publishers.

The Hebrew Prayer Book: 1, 26 from the Authorised Daily Prayer Book of the United Hebrew Congregations of the British Empire.

Marjorie Holmes: 46, 82, 103, 122 from *I've Got to Talk to Somebody, God* by Marjorie Holmes. Copyright © 1968, 1969 by Marjorie Holmes Mighell. Reproduced by permission of the publisher Hodder and Stoughton Limited. Permission sought from the Estate of the late Marjorie Holmes.

J. S. Hoyland: 124 from *The One Who Listens*, ed. Michael Hollings and Etta Gullick, published by McCrimmons, Great Wakering, Essex, 1971. Used with permission.

Christopher Idle: 176 from *Prayers for Today's Church*, ed. Dick Williams (London: Falcon Books/CPAS, 1972) with permission, <www.cpas.org.uk>.

Helen Jaeger: 50 from *As Night Falls* by Helen Jaeger, published by Lion Hudson plc, 1995. Copyright © 2005 Helen Jaeger. Used with permission of Lion Hudson plc.

Japanese Shinto: 52 from *Norito: a new translation of the ancient Japanese ritual prayers* by Donald L. Philippi (Tokyo: IJCC, 1959).

Kairos/Fr Mick Melvin: 37, 96, 100, 105, 115 from *Evening Prayer* by Kairos and RTE (Dublin: TownHouse, 2000).

B. A. Leary: 106 from *A Book of Prayers for Schools* by B. A. Leary, copyright © SCM Press. Used by permission of Hymns Ancient & Modern Ltd.

Dr Jim Lewis: 73 from the Baptist Memorial Hospital Chaplaincy Centre website.

Jeanne Lischer: 21 from *Women Pray*, ed. Karen L. Roller (New York: Pilgrim Press, 1986).

Phyllis Lovelock: 62 from *A Book of Childhood Prayers & Verses*, ed. Carolyn Martin (London: Hodder and Stoughton, 1983).

Nancy Martin: 19, 118 from *A Book of Childhood Prayers & Verses*, ed. Carolyn Martin (London: Hodder and Stoughton, 1983).

G. R. D. McLean: 173 from *Prayers of the Western Highlanders* by G. R. D. McLean (London: SPCK, 2008), by permission of SPCK.

Thomas Merton: 49 from *Thoughts in Solitude* by Thomas Merton. Copyright © Farrar, Straus and Giroux.

Eric Milner-White: 66 from *My God, My Glory* by Eric Milner-White (London: SPCK, 1954), by permission of SPCK.

Northumbria Community: 35, 42, 83, 88, 123, 140 from *Celtic Night Prayer*. Reprinted by permission of HarperCollins Publishers Ltd. © 1996 the Northumbria Community.

John O'Donohue: 137 from *Benedictus* by John O'Donohue, published by Bantam Press, 2007. Reprinted by permission of the Random House Group Ltd. From TO BLESS THE SPACE BETWEEN US: A BOOK OF BLESSINGS by John O'Donohue, copyright © 2008 by John O'Donohue. Used by permission of Doubleday, a division of Random House, Inc.

Michael Perry: 16, 20, 61 from *Bible Praying* by Michael Perry (London: Fount, 1992).

Jan Sutch Pickard: 71 'Gethsemane Prayer' from *Vice Versa* (Buxton: The Church in the Marketplace Publications, 1997), © Jan Sutch Pickard.

William Portsmouth: 53, 54, 98 from *Healing Prayer* by William Portsmouth (Evesham: Arthur James Ltd, 1954).

Prayers for Teenagers: 47, 72 from *Prayers for Teenagers*, ed. Nick Aiken (London: SPCK, 2003), by permission of SPCK.

Melissa Roberts: 78 by Melissa Roberts, <www.suite101.com>.

Anna Rogalski: 86.

Peter Rowlett: 11, 113, 120.

Virginia Salmon: 60 from *A Book of Childhood Prayers & Verses*, ed. Carolyn Martin (London: Hodder and Stoughton, 1983).

Albert Schweitzer: 92 from *God of a Hundred Names*, comp. and ed. Barbara Greene and Victor Gollancz (London: Victor Gollancz, 1962).

The Seafarers' Prayer Book: 74 by permission of the Apostleship of the Sea. Published by the Apostleship of the Sea, Herald House, Lamb's Passage, Bunhill Row, London EC1Y 8LE.

J. D. Searle: 178 from *Prayers for Today's Church*, ed. Dick Williams (London: Falcon Books/CPAS, 1972), with permission, <www.cpas.org.uk>.

Gilbert Shaw: 131 from *The Prayer Manual* by Gilbert Shaw (Mowbray), reproduced by kind permission of Continuum International Publishing Group.

Katharine Short: 95 from *Reflections: A Book for Mums* by Katharine Short (Oxford: Lion, 1981).

Ray Simpson: 152 from *Prayers of Calm* by Ray Simpson (Stowmarket: Kevin Mayhew, 2005). © Ray Simpson. Used by permission of Kevin Mayhew Ltd.

Lucy Smith: 107 from *Prayers for Today's Church*, ed. Dick Williams (London: Falcon Books/CPAS, 1972), with permission, <www.cpas.org.uk>.

Rita Snowden: 31, 51, 104, 155, 161 from *A Woman's Book of Prayers* (London: Collins Fount, 1980) and *Prayers in Later Life* (London: Collins Fount, 1980).

Dorothy M. Stewart: 10, 126, 150.

Margaret T. Taylor: 69 from *Encounters, the URC Prayer Handbook 1988*, published by the United Reformed Church and used with permission.

Corrie ten Boom: 147 from *The Five Silent Years of Corrie ten Boom* by Pamela Rosewell copyright © 1986 by the Zondervan Corporation. Used by permission of Zondervan Publishing House.

Beryl White: 25.

John Williamson: 132 from *A New Zealand Prayer Book/He Karakia Mihinare o Aotearoa* by the Anglican Church in New Zealand (Auckland: William Collins, 1989).

Patricia Wilson: 2, 70 reprinted from *Quiet Spaces: Prayer Interludes for Women* by Patricia Wilson. Copyright © 2002 by The Upper Room®. Used by permission from The Upper Room Books®. To order, phone 1.800.972.0433 or go to <www.upperroom.org/bookstore>.

Young Christians at Prayer: 171 from *Young Christians at Prayer* (London: SPG Youth and Education Department, 1961) by permission of USPG: Anglicans in World Mission.

Index of authors

Index of authors

Index of first lines

———◆———

Index of first lines